An Illustrated Rosary

Introduction & Meditations
by Fr Jonathan Martin

*Dedicated with affection to
His Holiness Pope John Paul II*

FAMILY PUBLICATIONS
OXFORD

*The author and the publisher gratefully acknowledge the assistance of Lionel Gracey
in selecting and locating the works of art reproduced in this booklet.*

Annunciation, Fra Angelico, © 1990 Museo di San Marco, Photo Scala, Florence
— courtesy of the Ministero Beni e Attività Culturali.
Visitation, Workshop of Duc de Berry, © Walters Art Museum, Baltimore.
Nativity, Geertgen tot Sint Jans, © The National Gallery, London.
Presentation in the Temple, Bellini, © 1997 Photo Scala, Florence.
Finding in the Temple, Martini, © Board of Trustees of the National Museums and
Galleries on Merseyside (Walker Art Gallery, Liverpool).
Baptism of the Lord, anon., © Richard Conrad OP.
Marriage at Cana, Giotto, © 1990 Photo Scala, Florence.
Sermon on the Mount, Fra Angelico, © 1990 Museo di San Marco, Photo Scala,
Florence — courtesy of the Ministero Beni e Attività Culturali.
Transfiguration, Duccio, © The National Gallery, London.
Abendmahl, Sieger Köder, © Sieger Köder
Agony in the Garden, Mantegna, © The National Gallery, London.
Scourging, Fernandez, Cofradía Penitencial de la Santa Vera Cruz, Valladolid.
Crowning with Thorns, style of Mostaert, © The National Gallery, London.
Carrying of the Cross, Ugolino di Nerio, © The National Gallery, London.
Crucifixion, Grünewald, © Musée d'Unterlinden Colmar, photo O. Zimmerman.
Resurrection, anon., Musée Municipal de Bernay.
Ascension, Giotto, © 1990 Photo Scala, Florence.
Descent of the Holy Spirit, Giotto, © 1990 Photo Scala, Florence.
Assumption of the Virgin, Filippino Lippi, © 1990 Santa Maria Sopra Minerva,
Photo Scala, Florence — courtesy of the Ministero Beni e Attività Culturali.
Coronation of the Virgin, Fra Angelico, © 1990 Galleria degli Uffizi, Photo Scala,
Florence — courtesy of the Ministero Beni e Attività Culturali.

ISBN 1-871217-39-3

published by
Family Publications
6a King Street, Oxford OX2 6DF
www.familypublications.co.uk

Foreword

This illustrated booklet on the Rosary is a welcome addition for reflection on the mysteries of Our Lord's life during this year of the Rosary. It has obviously been compiled with great care and devotion and I am delighted to see the illustrations and reflections on the new Mysteries of Light included within it.

To recite the Rosary is, of course, nothing other than to contemplate, with Mary, the face of Christ and I hope that many will be led into a deeper understanding and appreciation of the prayer of the Rosary through this booklet.

+ *Cormac Murphy-O'Connor*

Cardinal Cormac Murphy O'Connor
Archbishop of Westminster

The Most Holy Rosary of the Blessed Virgin Mary

In October 1978, scarcely two weeks after his election to the See of Peter, His Holiness, Pope John Paul II publicly declared his love of the Rosary of the Blessed Virgin Mary:

> The Rosary is my favourite prayer. A marvellous prayer! Marvellous in its simplicity and its depth. [. . .] It can be said that the Rosary is, in some sense, a prayer-commentary on the final chapter of the Vatican II Constitution *Lumen Gentium*, a chapter which discusses the wondrous presence of the Mother of God in the mystery of Christ and the Church. Against the background of the words *Ave Maria* the principal events of the life of Jesus Christ pass before the eyes of the soul. They take shape in the complete series of the joyful, sorrowful and glorious mysteries, and they put us in living communion with Jesus through – we might say – the heart of his Mother. At the same time our heart can embrace in the decades of the Rosary all the events that make up the lives of individuals, families, nations, the Church, and all mankind, our personal concerns and those of our neighbour, especially those who are closest to us, who are dearest to us. Thus the simple prayer of the Rosary marks the rhythm of human life.
>
> [*Angelus: Insegnamenti di Giovanni Paolo II*, I (1978): 75–76]

It was to mark the beginning of the twenty-fifth year of his Pontificate, and 'to counter a certain crisis of the Rosary', that Pope John Paul II issued the Apostolic Letter, *Rosarium Virginis Mariae* (RVM), setting again his own ministry within the daily rhythm of the Rosary and appealing to the whole Christian community to rediscover this prayer 'so easy and yet so rich' (*RVM* 43). It is to this end that he proclaimed the year from October 2002 to October 2003 the Year of the Rosary.

The Holy Father's Letter on the Rosary of the Virgin Mary will be remembered, perhaps above all, for the five new mysteries which it proposed be added to the traditional pattern. The Pope has selected these new 'Mysteries of Light' (or 'Luminous Mysteries') so that the Rosary might become more fully a 'compendium of the Gospel', by including the mysteries of Christ's public ministry between his Baptism and his Passion:

> Each of these mysteries of light is a revelation of the Kingdom now present in the very person of Jesus. His Baptism in the Jordan is first of all a mystery of light. Here, as Christ descends into the waters – the innocent one who became 'sin' for our sake (cf. *2 Corinthians* 5:21) – the heavens open wide and the voice of the Father declares him the beloved Son (cf. *Matthew* 3:17 and parallels), while the Spirit descends on him to invest him with the mission which he is to carry out.

> The second mystery of light is the first of the signs, given at Cana (cf. *John* 2:1–12), when Christ changes water into wine and opens the hearts of the disciples to faith, thanks to the intervention of Mary, the first among believers.

> The third mystery of light is the preaching by which Jesus proclaims the coming of the Kingdom of God, calls to conversion (cf. *Mark* 1:15) and forgives the sins of all who draw near to him in humble trust (cf. Mark 2:3–13; Luke 7:47–48): the inauguration of that ministry of mercy which he continues to exercise until the end of the world, particularly through the sacrament of Reconciliation which he has entrusted to his Church (cf. *John* 20:22–23).

> The mystery of light *par excellence* is the Transfiguration, traditionally believed to have taken place on Mount Tabor. The glory of the Godhead shines forth from the face of Christ as the Father commands the astonished disciples to 'listen to him' (cf. *Luke* 9:35 and parallels) and to prepare

to experience with him the agony of the Passion, so as to come with him to the joy of the Resurrection and a life transfigured by the Holy Spirit.

The final mystery of light is the institution of the Holy Eucharist, in which Christ offers his body and blood as food under the signs of bread and wine, and testifies 'to the end' his love for humanity (*John* 13:1), for whose salvation he will offer himself in sacrifice. [*RVM* 21]

The Rosary is 'an exquisitely contemplative prayer' (*RVM* 12). It is a way of 'remembering Christ with Mary' (*RVM* 13) who lived with her eyes fixed on Christ, treasuring his every word, and pondering them in her heart. (*Luke* 2:19) It is a form of prayer, quietly introducing and faithfully echoing the Sacred Liturgy, which 'trains in holiness those who pray it'.

As a form of contemplative prayer, the recitation of the Rosary cannot be rushed, nor seen only in terms of the prayers that are spoken. Pope Paul VI recognised this when he wrote:

> Without contemplation, the Rosary is a body without a soul, and its recitation runs the risk of becoming a mechanical repetition of formulas, in violation of the admonition of Christ: 'In praying do not heap up empty phrases as the Gentiles do; for they think they will be heard for their many words' (*Matthew* 6:7). By its nature, the recitation of the Rosary calls for a quiet rhythm and a lingering pace, helping the individual to meditate on the mysteries of the Lord's life as seen through the eyes of her who was closest to the Lord. In this way the unfathomable riches of these mysteries are disclosed.
> [Apostolic Exhortation *Marialis Cultus* (2 Feb 1974), 47]

It is for this very reason that Pope John Paul II writes about the dignity and importance of the various elements which combine to make up the recitation of the Rosary (*RVM* 29–38). The very announcement of each mystery opens up a scenario on which to focus our attention.

How to Say the Rosary

THE ROSARY is a form of vocal and mental prayer on the Mysteries of our Redemption, divided into fifteen decades.

The recitation of each decade is accompanied by meditation on one of the fifteen events or "mysteries."

The Mysteries consist of 3 groups pictured on pages 2, 3, and 4.

6. Meditate on 3rd Mystery, saying the "Our Father," ten "Hail Marys" and the "Glory Be."

7. Meditate on 4th Mystery, saying the "Our Father," ten "Hail Marys" and the "Glory Be."

5. Meditate on 2nd Mystery, saying the "Our Father," ten "Hail Marys" and the "Glory Be."

8. Meditate on 5th Mystery, saying the "Our Father," ten "Hail Marys" and the "Glory Be."

4. Meditate on 1st Mystery, saying the "Our Father," ten "Hail Marys" and the "Glory Be."

9. Concluding prayers, "Hail Holy Queen" and "Let us Pray: O God, whose only begotten Son, etc."

3. Say three "Hail Marys" and the "Glory Be."

2. Say the "Our Father."

1. Make the Sign of the Cross, say the Apostles' Creed.

The Family That Prays Together Stays Together

THE JOYFUL MYSTERIES

Mondays and Thursdays
Sundays of Advent
and after Epiphany until Lent.

1st Joyful Mystery
The Annunciation

The Angel Gabriel appears to Mary, announcing She is to be the Mother of God.

MARCH 25

5th Joyful Mystery
The Finding in the Temple

The Blessed Mother finds Jesus in the Temple.

FEAST OF THE HOLY FAMILY

2nd Joyful Mystery
The Visitation

Elizabeth greets Mary: "Blessed art Thou among women and blessed is the fruit of Thy womb!"

MAY 31

4th Joyful Mystery
The Presentation

The Blessed Mother presents the Child Jesus in the Temple.

FEBRUARY 2

3rd Joyful Mystery
The Nativity

The Virgin Mary gives birth to the Redeemer of the World.

DECEMBER 25

The pictures in this booklet, illustrating each of the mysteries of the Rosary, serve a similar function. Drawn from a number of sources and accompanied by short meditations, for both private and communal use, they help to direct the imagination and the mind towards the particular episodes in the life of Christ.

The announcement of the mystery is followed by a reading from the Sacred Scriptures, for 'no other words can ever match the efficacy of the inspired word' (*RVM* 30). In listening to this Biblical passage, which we recognise as being truly the word of God, we understand that it is spoken for today and spoken for us.

Silence is one of the secrets of contemplative prayer, and so it finds its place here, in the light of the word of God, so that he may be allowed to speak. It is the atmosphere in which our attention to the word of God and our meditation on the mystery concerned may be most effectively nourished (cf. *Catechism of the Catholic Church* 2709ff).

Only now is one ready to move into vocal prayer, raising the heart and mind, first of all, to the Father in the words which Jesus himself gave us. 'In each of his mysteries, Jesus always leads us to the Father ... He is continually turned towards him. He wants us to share in his intimacy with the Father, so that we can say with him: "Abba, Father" ' (cf. *CCC* 2759ff).

The ten Hail Marys are the most substantial element in the Rosary. The first half of this prayer echoes the words of Gabriel at the annunciation (the first joyful mystery); its answering phrase is the Church's trusting petition to the 'Mother of Mercy' for the help of her prayers (cf. *CCC* 2673–2679). The high point of this prayer, the centre on which these two parts hinge, is the holy name of Jesus, 'the name which is above all other names', and at whose mention 'all beings in the heavens, on earth and in the underworld should bend the knee' (*Philippians* 2:9–11). The holy name of Jesus, the 'centre of gravity' of the Hail Mary, should not be spoken hurriedly, for its very mention helps us to enter more deeply into the life of Christ.

Although *Rosarium Virginis Mariae* makes no mention of the prayer of Our Lady of Fatima, it has become common to include this petition to Jesus at the conclusion of each mystery. Given in 1917 to the three shepherd children by 'the Lady of the Rosary' this now well-known prayer (included in the introductory prayers of this booklet) was to be added to the offering of each mystery.

The Rosary may, of course, be recited in full every day 'In this way it fills with prayer the days of many a contemplative, or keeps company with the sick and the elderly who have abundant time at their disposal' (*RVM* 38). But, recognising that, for most of us, the daily recitation of all twenty mysteries of the Rosary would be too much, the Pope suggests the following pattern:

Joyful Mysteries	Monday and Saturday
Luminous Mysteries	Thursday
Sorrowful Mysteries	Tuesday and Friday
Glorious Mysteries	Wednesday and Sunday

As well as giving fresh life to the Rosary and enkindling renewed interest in this much loved (but sometimes 'wrongly devalued') path of contemplation, *Rosarium Virginis Mariae* comes as a timely plea to implore from God the gift of peace:

> The grave challenges confronting the world at the start of this new Millennium lead us to think that only an intervention from on high, capable of guiding the hearts of those living in situations of conflict and those governing the destinies of nations, can give reason to hope for a brighter future. [*RVM* 40]

The Rosary is also a prayer of and for the family, 'increasingly menaced by forces of disintegration', to which we need to return:

> Many of the problems facing contemporary families, especially in economically developed societies, result from their increasing difficulty in communicating. Families seldom manage to come together, and the rare occasions when they do are often taken up with watching television.

> To return to the recitation of the family Rosary means filling daily life with very different images, images of the mystery of salvation: the image of the redeemer, the image of his most Blessed Mother. The family that recites the Rosary together reproduces something of the atmosphere of the household of Nazareth: its members place Jesus at the centre, they share his joys and sorrows, they place their needs and their plans in his hands, they draw from him the hope and the strength to go on. [*RVM* 41]

In so many places, the Rosary is no longer taught to children and young people. This is a mistake which so often springs from an objection to the Rosary based on an impoverished method of praying it. But a 'positive, impassioned and creative' presentation of this most significant prayer is capable, with God's help, of achieving quite remarkable results, even a harvest of holiness amongst the young.

May this final appeal of the Pope, who has, throughout his Pontificate, entrusted himself completely to the protection of Our Lady, be answered enthusiastically and imaginatively by all who desire to enter deeply into the mystery of Jesus Christ, in company with his most Blessed Mother:

> I look to all of you, brothers and sisters of every state of life, to you Christian families, to you, the sick and elderly, and to you, young people: confidently take up the Rosary once again. Rediscover the Rosary in the light of Scripture, in harmony with the Liturgy, and in the context of your daily lives. [*RVM* 43]

Jonathan Martin
Our Lady of Lourdes, 2003

Introductory Prayers

The Sign of the Cross

In the name of ✠ the Father
and of the Son
and of the Holy Spirit.
Amen.

The Apostles' Creed

I believe in God, the Father almighty,
creator of heaven and earth.

I believe in Jesus Christ, his only Son, our Lord.
He was conceived by the power of the Holy Spirit
and born of the Virgin Mary.
He suffered under Pontius Pilate,
was crucified, died, and was buried.
He descended to the dead.
On the third day he rose again.
He ascended into heaven,
and is seated at the right hand of the Father.
He will come again to judge the living and the dead.

I believe in the Holy Spirit,
the holy Catholic Church,
the communion of saints,
the forgiveness of sins,
the resurrection of the body,
and the life everlasting.
Amen.

The Our Father

Our Father, who art in heaven,
hallowed be thy name.
Thy kingdom come.
Thy will be done on earth, as it is in heaven.
Give us this day our daily bread,
and forgive us our trespasses,
as we forgive those who trespass against us,
and lead us not into temptation,
but deliver us from evil.
Amen.

The Hail Mary

Hail, Mary, full of grace, the Lord is with thee;
blessed art thou among women,
and blessed is the fruit of thy womb, Jesus.
Holy Mary, Mother of God,
Pray for us sinners, now and at the hour of our death.
Amen.

The Glory be

Glory be to the Father, and to the Son, and to the Holy Spirit.
As it was in the beginning, is now, and ever shall be,
world without end.
Amen.

The Fatima prayer

O my Jesus,
forgive us our sins,
save us from the fires of hell.
Lead all souls to heaven,
especially those most in need of thy mercy.

The First Joyful Mystery

The Annunciation: Fra Angelico (c.1395–1445), Galleria degli Uffizi, Florence

The Annunciation

Scripture Reading   *Luke 1:26–38*

In the sixth month the angel Gabriel was sent by God to a town in Galilee called Nazareth, to a virgin betrothed to a man named Joseph, of the House of David; and the virgin's name was Mary. He went in and said to her, 'Rejoice, so highly favoured! The Lord is with you.' She was deeply disturbed by these words and asked herself what this greeting could mean, but the angel said to her, 'Mary, do not be afraid; you have won God's favour. Listen! You are to conceive and bear a son, and you must name him Jesus. He will be great and will be called Son of the Most High. The Lord God will give him the throne of his ancestor David; he will rule over the House of Jacob for ever and his reign will have no end.' Mary said to the angel, 'But how can this come about, since I am a virgin?' 'The Holy Spirit will come upon you,' the angel answered, 'and the power of the Most High will cover you with its shadow. And so the child will be holy and will be called Son of God. Know this too: your kinswoman Elizabeth has, in her old age, herself conceived a son, and she whom people called barren is now in her sixth month, for nothing is impossible to God.' 'I am the handmaid of the Lord,' said Mary, 'let what you have said be done to me.' And the angel left her.

Related texts: Is 7:10–14; Mt 1:18–25; CCC 422, 484ff

Silent Reflection

Meditation

How can it be that the eternal Word of God, the Alpha and Omega, the One to whom all time and all the ages belong, should take flesh in the womb of Mary, ever virgin? *Listen!* This mystery of God's love, foretold long ago, is sure and certain, for it is declared unto Mary by Gabriel, who stands in God's presence and bears from heaven the message of Immanuel – God *is* with us. And Mary, in her openness to this annunciation, conceives by the Holy Spirit.

Mary, Mother of our Saviour – *Pray for us*.

Our Father, ten Hail Marys, Glory be.

The Second Joyful Mystery

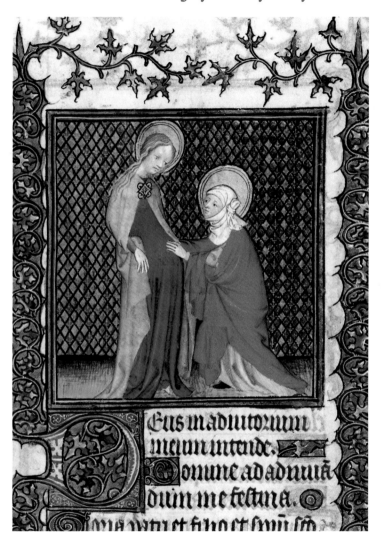

The Visitation: Workshop of Jean Duc de Berry (Book of Hours, late 14th Century), Walters Art Museum, Baltimore, USA

The Visitation

Scripture Reading *Luke 1:39–56*

Mary set out at that time and went as quickly as she could to a town in the hill country of Judah. She went into Zechariah's house and greeted Elizabeth. Now as soon as Elizabeth heard Mary's greeting, the child leapt in her womb and Elizabeth was filled with the Holy Spirit. She gave a loud cry and said, 'Of all women you are the most blessed, and blessed is the fruit of your womb. Why should I be honoured with a visit from the mother of my Lord? For the moment your greeting reached my ears, the child in my womb leapt for joy. Yes, blessed is she who believed that the promise made her by the Lord would be fulfilled.'

And Mary said, 'My soul proclaims the greatness of the Lord and my spirit exults in God my saviour; because he has looked upon his lowly handmaid. Yes, from this day forward all generations will call me blessed, for the Almighty has done great things for me. Holy is his name, and his mercy reaches from age to age for those who fear him. He has shown the power of his arm, he has routed the proud of heart. He has pulled down princes from their thrones and exalted the lowly. The hungry he has filled with good things, the rich sent empty away. He has come to the help of Israel his servant, mindful of his mercy – according to the promise he made to our ancestors – of his mercy to Abraham and to his descendants for ever.'

Mary stayed with Elizabeth about three months and then went back home.

Related texts: 2 Sam 6:1–15; Lk 1:67–79; CCC 495, 717

Silent Reflection

Meditation

The heart of this mystery lies in what cannot be seen, for beneath this joyful greeting is concealed a visitation from God to his people. Elizabeth, whom people called barren, adores the blessed fruit of Mary's womb; John the Baptist dances for joy, whirling round before the Lord. This double exchange is the cause of our joy.

Mary, Ark of the Covenant – *Pray for us.*

Our Father, ten Hail Marys, Glory be.

The Third Joyful Mystery

The Nativity: Geertgen tot Sint Jans (c. 1455–c. 1495), National Gallery, London

The Nativity

Scripture Reading *Luke 2:4–20*

So Joseph set out from the town of Nazareth in Galilee and travelled up
to Judaea, to the town of David called Bethlehem, since he was of David's
House and line, in order to be registered together with Mary, his
betrothed, who was with child. While they were there the time came
for her to have her child, and she gave birth to a son, her first-born. She
wrapped him in swaddling clothes, and laid him in a manger because
there was no room for them at the inn.

In the countryside close by there were shepherds who lived in the
fields and took it in turns to watch their flocks during the night. The
angel of the Lord appeared to them and the glory of the Lord shone
round them. They were terrified, but the angel said, 'Do not be afraid.
Listen, I bring you news of great joy, a joy to be shared by the whole
people. Today in the town of David a saviour has been born to you; he
is Christ the Lord. And here is a sign for you: you will find a baby
wrapped in swaddling clothes and lying in a manger.' And suddenly
with the angel there was a great throng of the heavenly host, praising
God and singing, 'Glory to God in the highest heaven, and peace to
men who enjoy his favour'.

Related texts: Is 9:1–7; Mt 2:1–18; Jn 1:1–5 & 9–14; CCC 525

Silent Reflection

Meditation

What wondrous child is this whom Mary beholds? Her prayer of
thanksgiving is echoed in heaven, for all creation gives glory to God.
All who make haste to kneel with Mary and see this thing that has
come to pass will be drawn from darkness and the shadow of death into
the way of holiness, light and peace.

Mary, Mystical Rose – *Pray for us.*

Our Father, ten Hail Marys, Glory be.

The Fourth Joyful Mystery

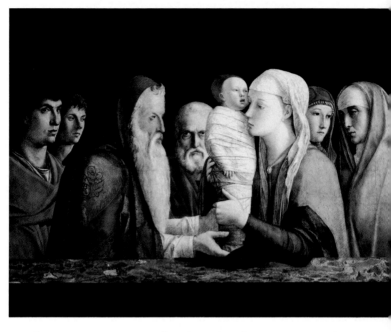

The Presentation: Giovanni Bellini (d.1516), Galleria Querini Stampalia, Venice

The Presentation of Christ in the Temple

Scripture Reading   *Luke 2:22–35*

And when the day came for them to be purified as laid down by the Law of Moses, they took him up to Jerusalem to present him to the Lord – observing what stands written in the Law of the Lord: Every first-born male must be consecrated to the Lord – and also to offer in sacrifice, in accordance with what is said in the Law of the Lord, a pair of turtledoves or two young pigeons. Now in Jerusalem there was a man named Simeon. He was an upright and devout man; he looked forward to Israel's comforting and the Holy Spirit rested on him. It had been revealed to him by the Holy Spirit that he would not see death until he had set eyes on the Christ of the Lord. Prompted by the Spirit he came to the Temple: and when the parents brought in the child Jesus to do for him what the Law required, he took him into his arms and blessed God; and he said, 'Now, Master, you can let your servant go in peace, just as you promised; because my eyes have seen the salvation which you have prepared for all the nations to see, a light to enlighten the pagans and the glory of your people Israel.'

As the child's father and mother stood there wondering at the things that were being said about him, Simeon blessed them and said to Mary his mother, 'You see this child: he is destined for the fall and for the rising of many in Israel, destined to be a sign that is rejected – and a sword will pierce your own soul too – so that the secret thoughts of many may be laid bare.'

Related texts: Num 18:15; Mal 3:1–4; Lk 2:36–40; CCC 529

Silent Reflection

Meditation

There is more for Mary to consider here, for pain and suffering are foretold. And what were merely swaddling bands of new birth, now speak of the wrappings of the grave. It is to Christ, this sign of contradiction, that all must look for light and salvation.

Mary, Queen of Prophets – *Pray for us.*

Our Father, ten Hail Marys, Glory be.

The Fifth Joyful Mystery

Christ Discovered in the Temple: Simone Martini (c. 1284–1344), Walker Art Gallery, Liverpool

The Finding of the Child Jesus in the Temple

Scripture Reading   *Luke 2:41–52*

Every year his parents used to go to Jerusalem for the feast of the Passover. When he was twelve years old, they went up for the feast as usual. When they were on their way home after the feast, the boy Jesus stayed behind in Jerusalem without his parents knowing it. They assumed he was with the caravan, and it was only after a day's journey that they went to look for him among their relations and acquaintances. When they failed to find him they went back to Jerusalem looking for him everywhere.

Three days later they found him in the Temple, sitting among the doctors, listening to them, and asking them questions; and all those who heard him were astounded at his intelligence and his replies. They were overcome when they saw him, and his mother said to him, 'My child, why have you done this to us? See how worried your father and I have been, looking for you.' 'Why were you looking for me?' he replied. 'Did you not know that I must be busy with my Father's affairs?' But they did not understand what he meant.

He then went down with them and came to Nazareth and lived under their authority. His mother stored up all these things in her heart. And Jesus increased in wisdom, in stature, and in favour with God and men.

Related texts: 1 Sam 2:26; Mt 23:1–12; Jn 7:14–18; CCC 534

Silent Reflection

Meditation

The joyful mysteries culminate in words spoken by the Word made flesh. From the silence of his hidden life, Jesus acknowledges the truth of what others have said of him. *For this I was born . . .* The truth of the double nature of this child is beyond our understanding, too. It is for our hearts to grasp in faith and love, that the Father's affairs – the mystery of his love – may be discerned in each and every scene of the Rosary.

Mary, Seat of Wisdom – *Pray for us.*

Our Father, ten Hail Marys, Glory be.

The First Mystery of Light

The Baptism of Christ: anon. (late 15th Century), Albi Cathedral, France

The Baptism of the Lord

Scripture Reading *Matthew 3:13–17*

Jesus came from Galilee to the Jordan to be baptised by John. John tried to dissuade him. 'It is I who need baptism from you,' he said, 'and yet you come to me!' But Jesus replied, 'Leave it like this for the time being; it is fitting that we should, in this way, do all that righteousness demands.' At this, John gave in to him.

As soon as Jesus was baptised he came up from the water, and suddenly the heavens opened and he saw the Spirit of God descending like a dove and coming down on him. And a voice spoke from heaven, 'This is my Son, the Beloved; my favour rests on him.'

Related texts: Gen 1:1–3; Ez 36:25–28; Mt 3:1–12; Mk 1:1–13; Lk 3:1–22; Jn 1:6–8, 15 & 19–34; CCC 535–537

Silent Reflection

Meditation

Christ stands at the threshold of his mission, illumined by the Creator of light. He who is the Beloved of the Father finds favour in Jordan's stream. 'Behold,' says John, 'the Lamb of God', the Saviour of the world. And he who must decrease in state reveals the Chosen One.

Mary, Mother of Divine Grace – *Pray for us.*

Our Father, ten Hail Marys, Glory be.

The Second Mystery of Light

The Wedding at Cana: Giotto (c.1266–1337), Scrovegni Chapel, Padua

The Wedding Feast at Cana

Scripture Reading *John 2:1–11*

There was a wedding at Cana in Galilee. The mother of Jesus was there, and Jesus and his disciples had also been invited. When they ran out of wine, since the wine provided for the wedding was all finished, the mother of Jesus said to him, 'They have no wine.' Jesus said, 'Woman, why turn to me? My hour has not come yet.' His mother said to the servants, 'Do whatever he tells you.' There were six stone water jars standing there, meant for the ablutions that are customary among the Jews; each could hold twenty or thirty gallons. Jesus said to the servants, 'Fill the jars with water,' and they filled them to the brim. 'Draw some out now,' he told them, 'and take it to the steward.' They did this; the steward tasted the water, and it had turned into wine. Having no idea where it came from – only the servants who had drawn the water knew – the steward called the bridegroom and said, 'People generally serve the best wine first, and keep the cheaper sort till the guests have had plenty to drink; but you have kept the best wine till now.'

This was the first of the signs given by Jesus: it was given at Cana in Galilee. He let his glory be seen, and his disciples believed in him.

Related texts: Mt 12:46–50; CCC 1613

Silent Reflection

Meditation

Taste and see that the Lord is good! At this first sign of his glory, the disciples are brought to faith. The wine that once was water announces God-made-man. May we come to share in the divinity of Christ, who humbled himself to share in our human nature.

Mary's reassuring words resonate in the hearts of all Christ's servants. In her company, all stewards of the mysteries of God proclaim the marvels worked by the Lord.

Mary, Help of Christians – *Pray for us*.

Our Father, ten Hail Marys, Glory be.

The Third Mystery of Light

Sermon on the Mount: Fra Angelico (c.1395–1445), Museo di San Marco, Florence

Christ's Proclamation of the Kingdom of God, with His Call to Conversion

Scripture Reading *Mark 1:14–15*

After John had been arrested, Jesus went into Galilee. There he proclaimed the Good News from God. 'The time has come,' he said, 'and the kingdom of God is close at hand. Repent, and believe the Good News.'

Related texts: Mt 5–7; 13:1–52; Lk 4:14–22; 9:57–62; 19:1–10, Jn 4:5–26; 8:2–12; 9:5; CCC 543

Silent Reflection

Meditation

The invitation to enter the kingdom of God is made through the preaching of Christ. His message of eternal life gladdens the heart. His commandments – inscribed on the tablet of the heart – give light to the eyes.

His words, which are both spirit and life, are alive and active now. They become the rock on which the wise man builds his house, and we are blessed if we heed this word and turn away from the darkness of sin.

The happiness of the Kingdom is within our grasp!

Thy kingdom come!

Mary, Mother of Christ – *Pray for us.*

Our Father, ten Hail Marys, Glory be.

The Fourth Mystery of Light

The Transfiguration: Duccio di Buoninsegna (c.1255–c.1319), National Gallery, London

The Transfiguration

Scripture Reading   *Luke 9:28–36*

Jesus took with him Peter and John and James and went up the mountain
to pray. As he prayed, the aspect of his face was changed and his clothing
became brilliant as lightning. Suddenly there were two men there talking
to him; they were Moses and Elijah appearing in glory, and they were
speaking of his passing which he was to accomplish in Jerusalem. Peter
and his companions were heavy with sleep, but they kept awake and
saw his glory and the two men standing with him. As these were leaving
him, Peter said to Jesus, 'Master, it is wonderful for us to be here; so let
us make three tents, one for you, one for Moses and one for Elijah'. –
He did not know what he was saying. As he spoke, a cloud came and
covered them with shadow; and when they went into the cloud the
disciples were afraid. And a voice came from the cloud saying, 'This is
my Son, the Chosen One. Listen to him.' And after the voice had
spoken, Jesus was found alone.

*Related texts: Ex 34:29–35; Deut 5:22–27; Mt 17:1–8; Mk 9:2–8;
Jn 1:14 & 16–18; CCC 554ff*

Silent Reflection

Meditation

The Light from Light stands framed in glory as Moses and Elijah point
to him who comes to complete their work. They speak of what is still
to be accomplished through love that knows no greater form.

But the voice which overshadows all is the voice of the One who
cannot be seen. And in his command to listen to Jesus we find the Way,
the Truth and the Life.

The splendour of this moment is not to be preserved nor are the
disciples to publish it abroad. But in its memory is found a glimpse of
those glorious mysteries through which the lives of all the disciples of
Jesus are transfigured.

Mary, Mother of Our Creator – *Pray for us.*

Our Father, ten Hail Marys, Glory be.

The Fifth Mystery of Light

The Last Supper: Sieger Köder (contemporary)

The Institution of the Eucharist as the Sacramental Expression of the Paschal Mystery

Scripture Reading   *Matthew 26:26–29*

Now as they were eating, Jesus took some bread, and when he had said the blessing he broke it and gave it to the disciples. 'Take it and eat,' he said, 'this is my body.' Then he took a cup, and when he had returned thanks he gave it to them. 'Drink all of you from this,' he said, 'for this is my blood, the blood of the covenant, which is to be poured out for many for the forgiveness of sins. From now on, I tell you, I shall not drink wine until the day I drink the new wine with you in the kingdom of my Father.'

Related texts: Ex 12:1–8 & 11–14; 16:4–5; Mk 14:12–25;
Lk 22:7–23; Jn 6:1–58; 13:1–35; 1 Cor 11:23–29; Rev 19:5–9;
CCC 1337ff

Silent Reflection

Meditation

'Do this in memory of me.'

How can we forget, with Christ still here in sacramental signs, the sacrifice he offered once for all upon the cross? In broken bread, his living body, and wine, his saving blood, we find the face of Christ our God, and look for his return.

On this night of shadows and betrayal, in the obscurity of that Upper Room, Christ gives his pledge of the life to come to all with eyes to see.

Mary, Mother of the Church – *Pray for us.*

Our Father, ten Hail Marys, Glory be.

The First Sorrowful Mystery

The Agony in the Garden: Andrea Mantegna (1430–1506), National Gallery, London

The Agony in the Garden

Scripture Reading   *Luke 22:39–47*

Jesus then left to make his way as usual to the Mount of Olives, with the disciples following. When they reached the place he said to them, 'Pray not to be put to the test.'

Then he withdrew from them, about a stone's throw away, and knelt down and prayed. 'Father,' he said, 'if you are willing, take this cup away from me. Nevertheless, let your will be done, not mine.' Then an angel appeared to him, coming from heaven to give him strength. In his anguish he prayed even more earnestly, and his sweat fell to the ground like great drops of blood.

When he rose from prayer he went to the disciples and found them sleeping for sheer grief. 'Why are you asleep?' he said to them. 'Get up and pray not to be put to the test.'

He was still speaking when a number of men appeared, and at the head of them the man called Judas, one of the Twelve.

Related texts: Gen 3:1–15;   Mt 26:30–56;   Mk 14:32–52;   Jn 18:1–11; CCC 612

Silent Reflection

Meditation

Your will be done! Schooled in this prayer from the lips of his mother, Jesus appeals to his Father in heaven. The anguish of this moment is real for, with his disciples asleep, Jesus is alone against the might of the world and the approaching moment of betrayal. But in this garden, on the Mount, Jesus, the Rock in whom alone all is sure, accepts the cross, the tree on which he will die.

Mary, Comforter of the Afflicted – *Pray for us.*

Our Father, ten Hail Marys, Glory be.

The Second Sorrowful Mystery

The Scourging: Gregorio Fernández (17ᵗʰ Century), Vera Cruz, Valladolid, Spain

The Scourging at the Pillar

Scripture Reading   *Mark 15:1–15*

First thing in the morning, the chief priests together with the elders and scribes, in short the whole Sanhedrin, had their plan ready. They had Jesus bound and took him away and handed him over to Pilate.

Pilate questioned him, 'Are you the king of the Jews?' 'It is you who say it,' he answered. And the chief priests brought many accusations against him. Pilate questioned him again, 'Have you no reply at all? See how many accusations they are bringing against you!' But, to Pilate's amazement, Jesus made no further reply.

At festival time Pilate used to release a prisoner for them, anyone they asked for. Now a man called Barabbas was then in prison with the rioters who had committed murder during the uprising. When the crowd went up and began to ask Pilate the customary favour, Pilate answered them, 'Do you want me to release for you the king of the Jews?' For he realised it was out of jealousy that the chief priests had handed Jesus over. The chief priests, however, had incited the crowd to demand that he should release Barabbas for them instead. Then Pilate spoke again. 'But in that case,' he said to them, 'what am I to do with the man you call king of the Jews?' They shouted back, 'Crucify him!' 'Why?' Pilate asked them, 'what harm has he done?' But they shouted all the louder, 'Crucify him!' So Pilate, anxious to placate the crowd, released Barabbas for them and, having ordered Jesus to be scourged, handed him over to be crucified.

Related texts: Mt 26:65–68; 27:11–26; Lk 23:1–25; Jn 18:19–24; 19:1; CCC 572

Silent Reflection

Meditation

It is love, not cord or rope, that binds Christ to this pillar of scourging. What have they done to him, those who bruised and battered his body as a foretaste of all that he would suffer on the cross?

Mary, Refuge of Sinners – *Pray for us.*

Our Father, ten Hail Marys, Glory be.

The Third Sorrowful Mystery

Christ Crowned with Thorns: style of Jan Mostaert (c.1472–1555), National Gallery, London

The Crowning with Thorns

Scripture Reading   *Matthew 27:27–31*

The governor's soldiers took Jesus with them into the Praetorium and collected the whole cohort round him. Then they stripped him and made him wear a scarlet cloak, and having twisted some thorns into a crown they put this on his head and placed a reed in his right hand. To make fun of him they knelt to him saying, 'Hail, king of the Jews!' And they spat on him and took the reed and struck him on the head with it. And when they had finished making fun of him, they took off the cloak and dressed him in his own clothes and led him away to crucify him.

Related texts: Is 53:2–5; Mk 15:16–20; Jn 18:33–19:16; CCC 615

Silent Reflection

Meditation

Parody and prophecy pervade this cruel coronation as the servants of earthly power pay mock homage to the sovereign king of heaven and earth! But the Sower of the word of God cannot be choked even by the agony of this moment and He who is perfectly obedient to the Father's will bears this shame and spitting in silence.

Mary, Mirror of Justice – *Pray for us*.

Our Father, ten Hail Marys, Glory be.

The Fourth Sorrowful Mystery

The Way to Calvary: Ugolino di Nerio (d. 1339/1349), National Gallery, London

The Carrying of the Cross

Scripture Reading *Luke 23:26–32*

As they were leading him away they seized on a man, Simon from Cyrene, who was coming in from the country, and made him shoulder the cross and carry it behind Jesus. Large numbers of people followed him, and of women too, who mourned and lamented for him. But Jesus turned to them and said, 'Daughters of Jerusalem, do not weep for me; weep rather for yourselves and for your children. For the days will surely come when people will say, "Happy are those who are barren, the wombs that have never borne, the breasts that have never suckled!" Then they will begin to say to the mountains, "Fall on us!"; to the hills, "Cover us!" For if men use the green wood like this, what will happen when it is dry?'

Related texts: Gen 22:1–14; Mt 10:38–39; 11:28–30; 16:24–25; 27:32–34; Mk 15:21–22; Jn 19:14–17; CCC 618, 1435, 2015, 2427

Silent Reflection

Meditation

There is much to recall from these steps to Calvary as Christ bears his cross to the place of the skull. In all these 'stations', Mary is there, fulfilling her role as Our Lady of Sorrows. In the silent exchange between Mother and Son time seems to pause for all that must pass in a single glance. But the urgency of this procession will brook no delay, so Christ and his cross are pushed and pulled, and dragged to the scene of our redemption.

Mary, Virgin most Merciful – *Pray for us.*

Our Father, ten Hail Marys, Glory be.

The Fifth Sorrowful Mystery

The Crucifixion: Matthias Grünewald (c. 1470–1528), Isenheim Altarpiece,
Musée d'Unterlinden, Colmar, France

The Crucifixion

Scripture Reading *Luke 23:33–38, 44–46*

When they reached the place called The Skull, they crucified him there and the two criminals also, one on the right, the other on the left. Jesus said, 'Father, forgive them; they do not know what they are doing.' Then they cast lots to share out his clothing.

The people stayed there watching him. As for the leaders, they jeered at him. 'He saved others,' they said, 'let him save himself if he is the Christ of God, the Chosen One.' The soldiers mocked him too, and when they approached to offer him vinegar they said, 'If you are the king of the Jews, save yourself.' Above him there was an inscription: 'This is the King of the Jews'.

It was now about the sixth hour and, with the sun eclipsed, a darkness came over the whole land until the ninth hour. The veil of the Temple was torn right down the middle; and when Jesus had cried out in a loud voice, he said, 'Father, into your hands I commit my spirit.' With these words he breathed his last.

Related texts: Mt 27:35–54; Mk 15:24–39; Jn 19:17–37; Phil 2:5–11; CCC 613, 614, 616

Silent Reflection

Meditation

In the darkest hour of all, the Light of the world is eclipsed by the shadow of death. Behold, the Lamb of God, who takes away the sins of the world! The Lord of Life surrenders himself to the hands of the Father, and dies.

'This is my body which will be given up for you . . .'

'This is my blood shed for you and for all so that sins may be forgiven . . .'

The sorrow of this mystery, pinned between heaven and earth, is the blade that cuts through Mary's soul. 'Behold, your mother!'

Mary, Virgin most Faithful – *Pray for us.*

Our Father, ten Hail Marys, Glory be.

The First Glorious Mystery

The Resurrection: English Sculpture (15ᵗʰ Century), Musée Municipal, Bernay, France

The Resurrection

Scripture Reading *Matthew 28:1–8*

After the Sabbath, and towards dawn on the first day of the week, Mary of Magdala and the other Mary went to visit the sepulchre. And all at once there was a violent earthquake, for the angel of the Lord, descending from heaven, came and rolled away the stone and sat on it. His face was like lightening, his robe white as snow. The guards were so shaken, so frightened of him, that they were like dead men. But the angel spoke; and he said to the women, 'There is no need for you to be afraid. I know you are looking for Jesus, who was crucified. He is not here, for he has risen, as he said he would. Come and see the place where he lay, then go quickly and tell his disciples, "He has risen from the dead and now he is going before you to Galilee; it is there you will see him". Now I have told you.' Filled with awe and great joy the women came quickly away from the tomb and ran to tell the disciples.

Related texts: Mk 16:1–14; Lk 24:1–44; Jn 20:1–29; 1 Cor 15:12–23; CCC 639–655

Silent Reflection

Meditation

Christ cannot be imprisoned in death for he is the Resurrection and the Life. There is no confinement for the one who fills the whole of creation. Truth bursts forth from the tomb, crushing indifference and waving aside all incredulity. This is the triumph of the cross, the source of blessing for all who believe. Do not be startled by this victorious mystery. Christ has conquered the world.

Mary, Queen of Peace – *Pray for us.*

Our Father, ten Hail Marys, Glory be.

The Second Glorious Mystery

The Ascension: Giotto (c.1266–1337), Scrovegni Chapel, Padua

The Ascension

Scripture Reading *Acts 1:6–14*

Now having met together, they asked him, 'Lord, has the time come? Are you going to restore the kingdom to Israel?' He replied, 'It is not for you to know times or dates that the Father has decided by his own authority, but you will receive power when the Holy Spirit comes on you, and then you will be my witnesses not only in Jerusalem but throughout Judaea and Samaria, and indeed to the ends of the earth.'

As he said this he was lifted up while they looked on, and a cloud took him from their sight. They were still staring into the sky when suddenly two men in white were standing near them and they said, 'Why are you men from Galilee standing here looking into the sky? Jesus who has been taken up from you into heaven, this same Jesus will come back in the same way as you have seen him go there.'

So from the Mount of Olives, as it is called, they went back to Jerusalem, a short distance away, no more than a sabbath walk; and when they reached the city they went to the upper room where they were staying; there were Peter and John, James and Andrew, Philip and Thomas, Bartholomew and Matthew, James son of Alphaeus and Simon the Zealot, and Jude son of James. All these joined in continuous prayer, together with several woman, including Mary the mother of Jesus.

Related texts: Mt 28:16–20; Mk 16:14–20; Lk 24:50–53; Eph 1:15–23; CCC 659–664

Silent Reflection

Meditation

Christ came from the Father. Now he leaves the world to go to the Father. Like the eyes of a servant on the hand of her mistress, so our eyes are on the Lord our God ... Who could not long to join him in that place which he has prepared? And so it is to heaven that we look for Christ to return to save us.

Mary, Gate of Heaven – *Pray for us.*

Our Father, ten Hail Marys, Glory be.

The Third Glorious Mystery

The Descent of the Holy Spirit: Giotto (c.1266–1337), Scrovegni Chapel, Padua

The Descent of the Holy Spirit

Scripture Reading   *Acts 2:1–12*

When Pentecost day came round, they had all met in one room, when suddenly they heard what sounded like a powerful wind from heaven, the noise of which filled the entire house in which they were sitting; and something appeared to them that seemed like tongues of fire; these separated and came to rest on the head of each of them. They were all filled with the Holy Spirit, and began to speak foreign languages as the Spirit gave them the gift of speech.

Now there were devout men living in Jerusalem from every nation under heaven, and at this sound they all assembled, each one bewildered to hear these men speaking his own language. They were amazed and astonished. 'Surely,' they said, 'all these men speaking are Galileans? How does it happen that each of us hears them in his own native language? Parthians, Medes and Elamites; people from Mesopotamia, Judaea and Cappadocia, Pontus and Asia, Phrygia and Pamphylia, Egypt and the parts of Libya round Cyrene; as well as visitors from Rome – Jews and proselytes alike – Cretans and Arabs; we hear them preaching in our own language about the marvels of God.' Everyone was amazed and unable to explain it; they asked one another what it all meant.

Related texts: Jn 16:7–14; Acts 1:12–14; 2:33–36; Gal 5:16–25; CCC 691, 731, 737

Silent Reflection

Meditation

In the privacy of their enclosure, the chosen Twelve are clothed from on high. To peer into that one room is to see the face of the Church, quickened by the outpouring of the Spirit and ready for the mission of evangelisation. This is the icon of our new life in Christ, lived out in the heart of the Church.

Mary, Queen of Apostles – *Pray for us.*

Our Father, ten Hail Marys, Glory be.

The Fourth Glorious Mystery

The Assumption: Filippino Lippi (c.1457–1504), S. Maria Sopra Minerva, Rome

The Assumption

Scripture Reading   *1 Thessalonians 4:13–18*

We want you to be quite certain, brothers, about those who have died, to make sure that you do not grieve about them, like the other people who have no hope. We believe that Jesus died and rose again, and that it will be the same for those who have died in Jesus: God will bring them with him. We can tell you this from the Lord's own teaching, that any of us who are left alive until the Lord's coming will not have any advantage over those who have died. At the trumpet of God, the voice of the archangel will call out the command and the Lord himself will come down from heaven; those who have died in Christ will be the first to rise, and then those of us who are still alive will be taken up in the clouds, together with them, to meet the Lord in the air. So we shall stay with the Lord for ever. With such thoughts as these you should comfort one another.

Related texts: Gen 5:23–24; 2 Kings 2:11; Ps 132:8; Is 62:10; Mt 25:1–13; 27:52–53; Lk 1:46–55; Jn 14:1–4; 1 Cor 15:51–57; CCC 966

Silent Reflection

Meditation

With what jubilation Mary is assumed into heaven! With sound of trumpet, lute and harp, with timbrel, dance, with strings and pipes, everything that lives and that breathes gives praise to God for his powerful deeds. To the accompaniment of all the choirs of heaven, Mary, the Mother of God, sings again *Magnificat*: 'The Almighty works marvels for me ... He casts the mighty from their thrones and raises the lowly ... '

Mary, Queen Assumed into Heaven – *Pray for us.*

Our Father, ten Hail Marys, Glory be.

The Fifth Glorious Mystery

Coronation of Our Lady: Fra Angelico (c.1395–1445), Galleria degli Uffizi, Florence

The Coronation of Our Lady and the Glory of all the Saints

Scripture Reading   *Revelation 12:1*

Now a great sign appeared in heaven: a woman, adorned with the sun, standing on the moon, and with the twelve stars on her head for a crown.

Related texts: Ex 20:12; 2 Tim 4:8; Rev 12:1–17; 21:2–4; 22:13–14; CCC 972

Silent Reflection

Meditation

In the solemn moment of Our Lady's coronation, heaven is radiant with joy. The handmaid of the Lord is crowned with honour by Christ, the Universal King. And she, who has kept her eyes fixed on him, shines forth as Queen of Heaven.

All generations call Mary blessed, imploring her help and protection. For she who has received the crown of righteousness, the crown of life, and the crown of glory, promised to all the disciples of Christ, prays for us all, pleading for grace.

Mary, Queen of all Saints – *Pray for us.*

Our Father, ten Hail Marys, Glory be.

Concluding Prayers

Hail, Holy Queen, Mother of mercy.
Hail, our life, our sweetness, and our hope.
To thee do we cry, poor banished children of Eve;
to thee do we send up our sighs,
mourning and weeping in this vale of tears.
Turn, then, most gracious advocate,
thine eyes of mercy toward us;
and after this our exile,
show unto us the blessed fruit of thy womb, Jesus.
O clement, O loving, O sweet Virgin Mary.

V. Pray for us, O Holy Mother of God.
R. That we may be made worthy of the promises of Christ.

Let us pray.

O God, whose only-begotten Son
by his life, death and resurrection
has purchased for us the rewards of eternal life;
grant, we beseech thee,
that meditating on these Mysteries
of the most holy Rosary of the Blessed Virgin Mary
we may both imitate what they contain
and obtain what they promise,
through the same Christ our Lord.
Amen.

The Litany of Loreto

Lord, have mercy.

Christ, have mercy.

Lord, have mercy.

Christ, hear us.

God the Father of heaven

God the Son, Redeemer of the world

God the Holy Spirit

Holy Trinity, one God

Lord, have mercy.

Christ, have mercy.

Lord, have mercy.

Christ, graciously hear us.

Have mercy on us.

Have mercy on us.

Have mercy on us.

Have mercy on us.

Holy Mary

Holy Mother of God

Holy Virgin of virgins

Mother of Christ

Mother of the Church

Mother of divine grace

Mother most pure

Mother most chaste

Mother inviolate

Mother undefiled

Mother most lovable

Mother most admirable

Mother of good counsel

Mother of our Creator

Mother of our Saviour

Virgin most prudent

Virgin most venerable

Virgin most renowned

Virgin most powerful

Virgin most merciful

Virgin most faithful

Pray for us.

etc.

Mirror of justice
Seat of wisdom
Cause of our joy
Spiritual vessel
Vessel of honour
Singular vessel of devotion
Mystical rose
Tower of David
Tower of ivory
House of gold
Ark of the Covenant
Gate of heaven
Morning star
Health of the sick
Refuge of sinners
Comforter of the afflicted
Help of Christians
Queen of angels
Queen of patriarchs
Queen of prophets
Queen of apostles
Queen of martyrs
Queen of confessors
Queen of virgins
Queen of all saints
Queen conceived without original sin
Queen assumed into heaven
Queen of the most Holy Rosary
Queen of the family
Queen of peace

Lamb of God, you take away the sins of the world
  Spare us, O Lord.
Lamb of God, you take away the sins of the world
  Graciously hear us, O Lord.
Lamb of God, you take away the sins of the world
  Have mercy on us.

Pray for us, O holy Mother of God.
  That we may be made worthy of the promises of Christ.

Let us pray.

Grant that we your servants, Lord,
may enjoy unfailing health of mind and body,
and through the prayers of the ever-blessed Virgin
Mary in her glory,
free us from our sorrows in this world,
and give us eternal happiness in the next,
through Christ Our Lord. *Amen.*